Handmade
Lacé®
Greetings Cards

*For my Rock, thank you for your incredibly
generous nature and for whisking me off on
exciting adventures in foreign lands. I L You!!!*

*For my Mum, Gran and Aunty Carol. These
three extraordinary women have in so many
ways past and present shaped, encouraged and
inspired my creative journey.*

Handmade
Lacé®
Greetings Cards

Melanie Hendrick

SEARCH PRESS

First published in Great Britain 2003

Search Press Limited
Wellwood, North Farm Road,
Tunbridge Wells, Kent TN2 3DR

Reprinted 2003

Text copyright © Melanie Hendrick
Photographs by Roddy Paine Photographic Studios
Photographs and design copyright © Search Press Ltd. 2003

Lacé is a registered trademark of Kars & Co b.v.

ISBN 1 903975 81 6

If you have difficulty obtaining any of the equipment or
materials mentioned in this book, please visit our website at
www.searchpress.com.

Alternatively, you can write to the Publishers, at the address
above, for a current list of stockists, including firms which
operate a mail-order service.

Publishers' note
All the step-by-step photographs in this book feature the
author, Melanie Hendrick, demonstrating how to make
handmade greetings cards. No models have been used.

Cover
Memory Lane Tag Book

Page 1
You're a Star Greetings Card

Page 3
Butterfly Dreams Card

Page 5
Oriental Bookmark

Printed in Spain by Elkar S. Coop., Bilbao 48012

ACKNOWLEDGEMENTS
Not enough space and so many to thank!
*To Marianne Perlot for supporting my use of the
Lacé line; Kars Holland for their generous
contribution of wonderful craft products including
Lacé; and special thanks to Betty Mulder for
sending me the Déjà Views paper assortment used
in the Floral Romance project – all your help and
enthusiasm is appreciated.*
*My heartfelt thanks to Sue Taylor of Craftwork
Cards for her innovative approach to blank card,
and for sending me enough to set up a shop!*
*To Irene and Hazel at S For Stamps for showering
me with stamps and for their wonderful creative
support of my mad stamp ideas! To Woodware for
Peel-Off eyelets.*
*To the Hickey family: Merve for cooking the best
risotto on the planet, Owen for giving up his new
bed, Matt for having really cool trousers and Jules
for her friendship, creative belief and
chauffeuring availability!*
*To my workshop participants at Millers and S For
Stamps for demanding not only beginner and
intermediate but also advanced Lacé technique
workshops, encouraging me to develop new ways
with Lacé!*
*A huge thanks to Roddy: you have done such a
beautiful job of photographing my projects, and
the author photo is not bad either!*
*Last but not least the Search Press team: Roz,
thanks for the opportunity to create book number
two; Sophie, thanks for being such an enthusiastic
editor and fellow paper addict; and finally Juan,
thanks for encouraging my input during
photography and for doing such a stunning job on
the front cover!*
*A special thanks to you the reader: without you
my dream of creating books would remain just
that – a dream.*

Contents

Introduction

As a creative person I am always on the lookout for something new to keep my cards fresh and innovative. So you can imagine my excitement when a friend from Holland sent me a couple of bright green templates with matching tools, a technique book in Dutch and a note to encourage me to have a go at Lacé, which was becoming a popular craft technique in Europe.

At first I was a little perplexed, as I don't read Dutch, but my curiosity got the better of me and I quickly became hooked. The Lacé technique began to dominate my card making, mixing perfectly with my addiction to rubber stamping and other papercrafts.

The term Lacé comes from a French word meaning 'linked together'. It began as a selection of products, but because of its popularity it has evolved into a technique of its own. Lacé involves cutting the template designs from two-toned paper, card or vellum. When you fold the cut flaps over, they reveal the contrasting colour. You then tuck each flap under the piece in front to create that 'linked together' effect.

Use the Lacé technique to enhance your favourite papercrafting techniques such as rubber stamping, 3D découpage, quilling or teabag folding, or as a beautiful embellishment down the spine of a card. No matter how you use this technique, you are guaranteed to create stunning cards that will delight the recipient and bring you hours of fun and delight in the creation.

Get ready to embark on a new creative adventure. Happy creating!

6

Materials

Lacé is essentially a cutting system, and therefore each component plays an important role in the execution of the technique.

Lacé templates and low tack tape

These are bright green and are made from quality metal. They are a real investment. I store mine in plastic transparent sleeves in a ring binder for convenience. Use low tack tape to secure the templates to the card, so that when you lift the tape off, it doesn't tear the surface of the card.

Lacé knife and spare blades

This knife is vital to the Lacé technique – any other craft knife would damage the templates. The blade is made at a 45° angle for precision cutting, and is wafer thin to glide through the template openings. The knife comes with spare blades, which are also available separately. Replace a blade when the point snaps or the blade starts to tear at the card or paper when cutting.

Lacé score and fold tool

This clever tool is used to score the base cuts to make perfect hinges. The tool is then flipped over to the fold end to fold the hinge flat. The tool is also handy for applying glue: simply dip the scoring end into the glue tub and apply a dot to the card, then stick on a seed bead.

The Lacé kit: Lacé templates, cutting mat, knife and spare blades, score and fold tool, ruler and low-tack tape.

Lacé ruler

Tiny 11.5cm (4½in) heavy duty plastic ruler with a metal edge. This is handy for scoring or measuring, and with its metal edge, great for cutting areas you have missed.

Lacé cutting mat

A self-healing transparent cutting mat with clearly marked grid lines to help you line up your card and templates.

Duo card

This is a range of card and paper that is coloured differently on each side. It is available in a sumptuous range of metallic, pearlescent and plain colours. It is the duo card you choose to use with the Lacé technique that creates the impact when each cut is scored and folded.

Other cards and papers

Paper and card is something I can never have enough of. I store it lovingly by colour and size ready for inspiration to strike at any time! I also find it fun to create my own duo paper and card using the following assortment of cards and papers.

Vellum A lightweight translucent paper available in plain or printed colours. It is easy to cut for those of you who suffer from arthritis or find duo card too thick to cut through.

A selection of duo card

Printed papers Nowadays printed papers are as varied as fabric. Layer them over your cards as patterned backgrounds, or tear and collage them as accents.

Card blanks Thanks to the popularity of handmade cards, the shape, size and colour of card blanks available is staggering. I like to fold my own card blanks from A4 sheets as well as using ready-made sizes for ease and convenience.

Vellums, printed papers, cards and card blanks

Adhesive-backed matt paper

A single-sided paper used as a background paper. Peel off the backing and stick it to the card – no waiting for glue to dry!

Rubber stamps and inkpads

Used for creating instant images. These designs are mounted on to a clear acrylic block for precision stamping. I have used a mixture of dye-based inks for quick drying and pigments for directly colouring background papers.

Adhesive-backed matt paper, rubber stamps and inkpads

Coluzzle templates, knife and mat

Clear plastic, nested templates used for cutting apertures in different sizes in card or paper. The Coluzzle knife is a swivel knife that rotates 360°. It has a special plastic guard that acts as a guide when cutting a channel and prevents the blade from slipping. The Coluzzle mat is essential to the system. This is made from a plastic foam material and allows the knife to cut freely.

Coluzzle templates and a Coluzzle knife and mat are shown here with some of the shapes you can create using them.

Decorative items

Peel-Off eyelets are clever faux eyelets that give the impression of metal but are quick and easy to use.

Wire The higher the gauge, the finer the wire. Use 18 gauge for jump rings and clips, and 26 gauge for crimping and detail work.

Invest in good quality **threads** for machine stitching as they can provide the finishing touch that really sets off your card.

Collect unusual **buttons** from antique or second-hand shops or holiday markets.

Seed beads are tiny single hole beads made from plastic or metal.

Metal eyelets and charms are available in a huge range of colours.

Sheer ribbon has a beautiful translucent quality and **velvet ribbon** adds an heirloom quality to concertina and tag books.

3D pearlescent paint dries raised – useful for accents such as dots.

Embroidery scissors Keep these for cutting thread only and they should last a lifetime.

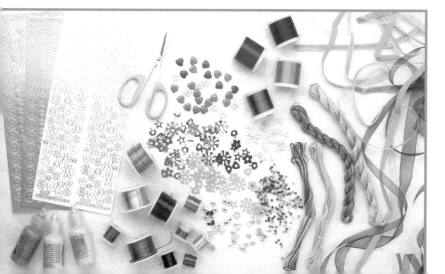

Peel-Off eyelets, 18g and 26g wire, embroidery threads, machine threads, seed beads, eyelet charms, buttons, velvet and sheer ribbon and embroidery scissors

Other materials

Wire cutters and round-nosed pliers are used for shaping and cutting wire. For safety, never cut wire anywhere near your eyes.

A **permanent pen** is useful for marking a reference point on your template.

Keep a **fine lead pencil** for designing your own templates and marking measurements.

A 3mm ($^1/_8$in) **single hole punch** is the perfect size for punching a hole in a card and then adhering a Peel-Off eyelet.

An **eyelet tool set** consists of a hole maker and an eyelet setter. Position the hole maker, hammer twice with a **mini hammer**, feed the eyelet through the hole, flip the card over, then position the eyelet setter into the eyelet and hammer flat.

Keep **plastic tubes** in different sizes for wrapping wire around to make paper clips.

These large and small **paper scissors** are my favourites. They have shear style handles that are perfect for large hands.

A **metal ruler** is ideal for cutting with a craft knife.

A **paper trimmer** is a handy mini-guillotine, useful for those of us who have trouble cutting straight! Feed paper or card under the weight and slide the blade one way for a perfect cut.

A **paper crimper** with metal cogs is good for making crimped wire. Feed 26 gauge wire through the cogs and turn the handle.

Craft punches are great for producing identical repeat designs. Position card or paper in the opening, press the button and punch out the design.

My **sewing machine** is my secret adhesive! Heavy-duty needles are best for stitching through layers of vellum, card or paper.

I use **high tack glue** for sticking beads and embellishments to cards. Good quality high tack glue should go on opaque and dry clear.

3D foam squares are tiny double-sided sticky pads with a foam core, used to raise an image from the background.

Double-sided tape is used for mounting layers of paper and card on to base card.

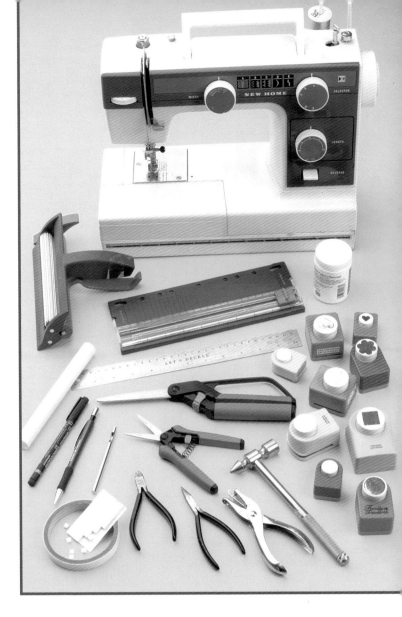

Further materials for making Lacé cards, including a sewing machine, high tack glue, craft punches, mini hammer, single hole punch, round-nosed pliers and wire cutters, double-sided tape, 3D foam squares, pencil and permanent marker, small and large paper scissors, eyelet tool set, tube, metal ruler, paper trimmer and crimper.

Basic techniques

The Lacé technique is not for quick card making. Time must be taken, combined with a little know-how, to achieve the beautiful Lacé effect. 'Practise' and 'relax' are words I recall from when I first started working with the Lacé knife. Since the blade is cut at a 45° angle, it is important to hold it at that angle when applying pressure, so that you cut cleanly through your card. If you can get the cutting right, the rest of the steps flow easily.

You will need

Lacé template 3
Lacé knife and spare blades
Lacé score and fold tool
Lacé ruler
Lacé cutting mat
Low tack tape
Card blanks
Permanent marker

1. Open your card blank and place it on your Lacé cutting mat. Position the template on the open card. Centre the template on the front and secure it with low tack tape. Mark the template with a reference point, so that you will know where you started cutting.

2. Put the Lacé knife in at a 90° angle. Punch the tip of the blade through the card to the cutting mat.

3. Relax the position in which you are holding the knife, until you are holding it as you would a pen.

4. Apply pressure and cut along the line in the template. At the end of it bring the knife up to a 90° angle again.

5. Rotate the cutting mat and start the other side of the cut, holding the knife at a 90° angle again. Go round the template cutting all the V shapes in the same way, ending at your reference mark, where you started.

6. Remove the template to reveal your cut design.

7. Position the Lacé ruler at the base of one of your cut shapes, so that it joins up the base cuts, and use the Lacé score and fold tool to score a line.

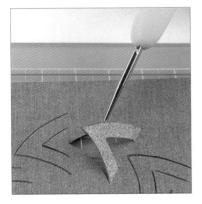

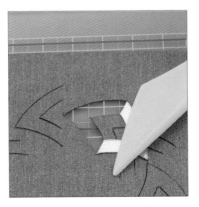

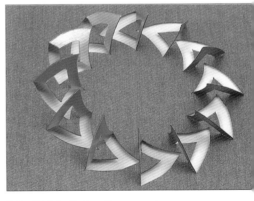

8. Lift up the flap with the same tool.

9. Flip the score and fold tool over and fold the flap with the other end.

10. Fold all the flaps up in the same way.

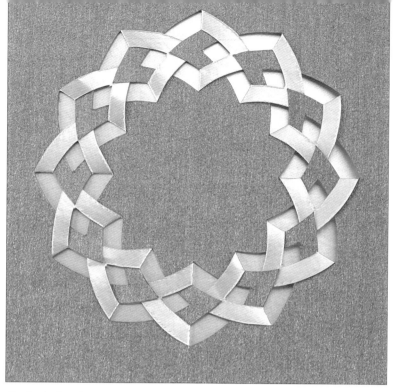

11. Tuck each folded back flap under the flap behind it.

The finished card

Using templates 2–21

Templates 2–21 have been made to be used as you see them. Simply follow the cutting lines. What makes these templates fun to work with is that they are available in a wonderful assortment of designs, producing very individual results.

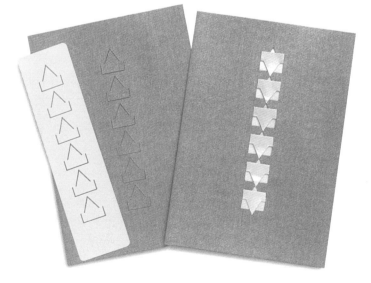

This bookmark template 21 has been used to decorate the spine of a card.

Template 12 is a flip and fold bookmark template, shown here with a cut card and a second card showing the flipped and folded effect.

Template 5 with the cut and folded results

Template 6 with a cut card, and a second card showing the camera aperture effect produced by folding

Using templates 22–34

Templates 22–34 have been designed so that you can be really creative with them. Use them as you see them, or try skipping some of the cutting lines to create thicker folds, or a combination of thick and thin folds. With one template you can create multiple results.

All these results were produced using template 27. On the left is a card showing the cutting lines before folding – you can see that some of the cutting lines have been skipped. How many variations can you come up with?

Kiss Card

You are now ready to make your first kiss card (KISS stands for Keep it Short and Simple)! I like a challenge and I really enjoy making cards that are visually interesting. It goes without saying that the Lacé technique achieves just that – but what happens when you apply that principle to the main card, rather than making separate Lacé artwork?

This card is modern, fun and easy to achieve.

You will need

Lacé template 26, knife and spare blades, score and fold tool, ruler and cutting mat

Low tack tape

A4 olive-coloured duo card and scrap card the same colour

Square craft punches: small (6mm/¼in), medium (13mm/½in) and large (25mm/1in)

Beads

High tack glue

Metal ruler

1. Score and fold a sheet of A4 olive-coloured duo card in half.

Tip

Use the score and fold tool to make a professional folded spine on your main card. This tool is also brilliant for applying tiny dots of high tack glue.

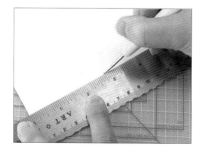

2. Turn the paper over to show the white side. Find the centre of the front and mark it at the top and bottom with the scoring tool.

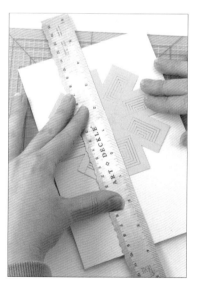

3. Align the scored marks with the centre mark of the template. Secure template in the position shown with low tack tape.

4. Open the card. Score from the top of the template to the tip of the card and from the bottom of the template to the bottom of the card.

5. On the right-hand side of your central score line only, cut the outline of the template.

6. Begin cutting at your reference point, skipping some lines to create a pattern.

7. Cut the next block on the template.

8. Continue cutting all the way round and remove the template.

9. Fold back the card on the score line at the centre of the front. Use the folding tool to make a good crease.

10. Score the bases of your cut shapes from the outside in from end line to end line. Then skip one, score the next one and so on.

11. Flip up and fold back the cut shapes.

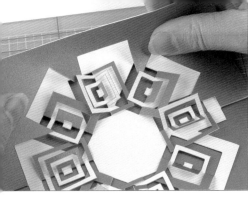

12. Hide the jagged parts of the outline by tucking them under the raised parts of the pattern.

13. Open the card out.

14. Line the template up with the edge and corner of the card. Hold it in place and cut the corner shape.

15. Cut all four corners in the same way.

16. Punch squares from scrap olive-coloured duo card: one large, five medium and five small.

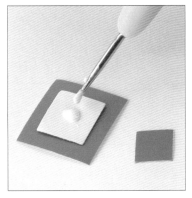

17. Use the scoring tool and high tack glue to stick a medium square, white side up, to the large square, and then a small square, olive side up, to the white square.

18. Stick the small olive squares to the medium squares, white side up. Dot on glue and stick on a bead.

19. Apply dots of high tack glue to the corners and stick a small beaded square to each. Place the large square in the centre. Stick beads above the middle of each side and one in the centre.

The finished Kiss card. If you are stuck for card ideas for the men in your life, this is perfect. With its gorgeous olive colour and modern feel it will make any shop-bought card hide!

Using different templates and coloured duo card creates a fresh look to this project every time. Try using the same technique to make funky place cards to enhance your table décor at parties.

20

Floral Romance

It is the paper and card combinations that make the Lacé technique so beautiful and unique.

In this project we make our own duo card by layering soft floral printed vellum and plaid printed paper over plain card to create a soft and romantic feel to our greetings card.

I am a bit of an embellishments addict and I like to personalise or theme my cards by incorporating metallic eyelets, eyelet charms and punched shapes.

This is an occasions card that says 'I cared enough to make it myself'.

You will need

Lacé template 25, knife and spare blades, score and fold tool, ruler and cutting mat

Low tack tape

White card blank, 14.5cm (5¾in) square

Vellum sleeve, 14.5 x 29cm (5¾ x 11½in)

Printed paper spine, 14.5 x 6.5cm (5¾ x 2½in)

Flower craft punch and green card

3mm (⅛in) single hole punch

Eyelet tool set and mini hammer

Eyelets and charms

Double-sided tape

Tip

Vellum does not need scoring as it folds easily, and it is easy to cut for people who have arthritis or other problems with their hands.

1. Fold the vellum to match the card blank and cut the printed paper for the spine. Fold the spine lengthwise at 38mm (1½in) in from the side.

2. Open the vellum and soften the spine so that it sits flat. Position the plaid printed paper spine as a guide, to show the space that will be left on the front of the card. Place the template in the centre of this space and stick it down.

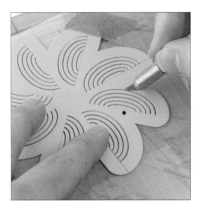

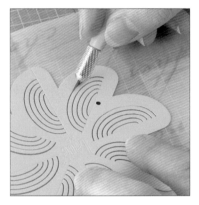

Tip

If you do not rotate the cutting mat when you have cut half-way round a curve in this way, you will end up with a point in the middle of the curve.

3. Cut a curved line to the centre of the curve only.

4. Rotate the cutting mat with the knife still in place and cut the second half of the curve.

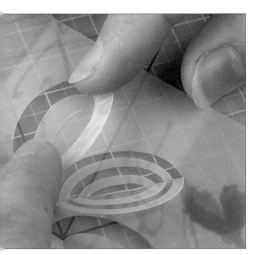

5. Cut all the curves in the same way. Fold up every other petal shape from the outside in, moving anti-clockwise round the flower.

6. Fold the petals down flat with the folding tool.

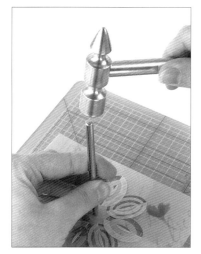

7. With the card, vellum and spine together, open the card. Take the 3mm ($^1/_8$in) single hole punch, centre it at the bottom of the spine, feed it in as far as it will go and punch through the front only. Punch the top of the spine in the same way.

8. Punch out two tiny daisies from green card and punch a hole in the centre of each using the single hole punch.

9. Place the vellum only on the cutting mat and use the hole maker from the eyelet set and the mini hammer to make a hole in the centre of the Lacé flower.

10. Take an eyelet charm and eyelet, fit them together and put them in the hole. Turn the vellum over, take the eyelet setter and hammer it to set the eyelet.

11. Put an eyelet, charm and punched daisy together and push them into one of the punched holes in the spine. Hammer them in and repeat with the other spine hole.

12. Stick a length of double-sided tape to the inside of the back of the spine and stick it to the back of the card.

The finished Floral Romance card. Experiment with duo card combinations, using the same techniques shown in this project. I really like the effect created by using a white card, as it highlights the patterns and colour of the printed vellum. Mixing and matching embellishments carries on the colour theme and brings an elegant harmony to the card.

These cards remind me of precious books with their decorated spines. By changing the spine embellishments, you alter the character of the card. I have heard that a picture paints a thousand words, so use hearts to say 'I love you' or to send a secret Valentine. Send stars for congratulations and daisies to say 'Thank you' or simply 'I'm thinking of you'. Make matching gift tags to dress up a parcel, or slot a bookmark into a book to make an extra special gift.

Old Shanghai

Lacé really lends itself to being used in conjunction with other papercrafts or general craft techniques. As a rubber stamper, my first thought was 'how can I mix the Lacé technique with rubber stamping?' I had hours of fun experimenting, and one of my favourite combinations is to mix pre-printed vellum with hand-stamped frames and background papers.

I have used pigment inks to colour and stamp because they are vibrant and creamy, and black dye-based ink because it is perfect for capturing the detail in the lady stamp.

My secret weapon is adhesive-backed matt paper, which is a dream to colour and easy to mount. Peel off the backing paper and adhere to your card – there is no need to set it aside to dry. You can also layer it over other colours to achieve a patterned fabric effect without giving a bulky feel to the card.

Another gadget I really like to use is the Coluzzle cutting system. The templates come in many different shapes. I like working with the circle as I can't cut a rounded shape freehand to save my life. The system gives instant results and is great for cutting apertures, frames and borders.

You will need

Lacé template 13, knife and spare blades, score and fold tool, ruler and cutting mat

Low tack tape

A4 pearlescent light purple card, folded

Dark purple card, 153mm x 203mm (6 x 8in)

Raspberry card, 128 x 178mm (5 x 7in)

Adhesive-backed matt paper

A4 printed vellum

Paper trimmer

Peel-Off eyelets

Coluzzle template: circle

Coluzzle knife and mat

Lady and flower rubber stamps

Inkpads

Daisy craft punch

3mm (1/8in) single hole punch

26 gauge wire and wire cutters

Paper crimper

3D foam squares

Scissors

High tack glue

Tip

Rubber stamp several background papers in one sitting so that you have them to hand when inspiration strikes!

1. Cut the purple and raspberry cards to the sizes given above.

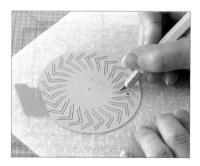

2. Centre the template on the front of the vellum, towards the top left-hand corner, stick it down with low tack tape and begin cutting at the reference mark.

28

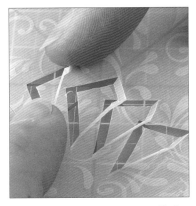 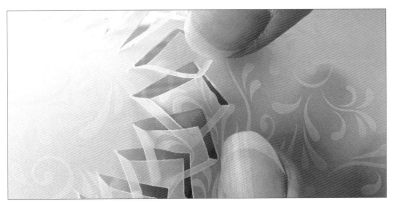

3. When you have cut all the way round, fold back every other triangle.

4. Tuck each folded back triangle under the triangle behind it.

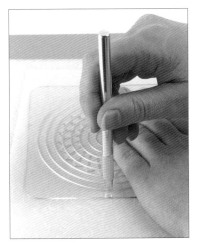  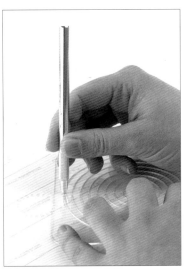

5. Position the circular Coluzzle template so that it frames the Lacé cutting. Take a Coluzzle knife. Make sure the blade is facing away from you and is at 90° to the work surface. Cut a semi-circle.

6. Cut the other half of the circle and snip the gaps to release the Lacé circle. Set it aside.

7. Place the Coluzzle circle template on a sheet of adhesive-backed matt paper and cut the outside track, then the next track in, to make a circular frame and an inner circle. Set these aside.

8. Measure two strips 38mm (1½in) wide and two strips 20mm (¾in) wide from adhesive-backed matt paper. Cut them with the paper trimmer. Start a little bit in from the edge.

9. Place one of the wider strips on scrap paper and wipe over it with an inkpad to colour it.

10. The wider strips should be coloured with a purple inkpad and the narrower ones with a pink inkpad.

11. Stamp the purple strips and circle frame with a flower design and a black inkpad. Stamp the pink ones in magenta ink first and then use peony ink with a larger flower stamp.

12. Colour the previously set aside circle with the purple inkpad, then stamp it with the lady stamp in black dye-based ink. Add a flower stamp as shown. Cut round the lady shape with scissors.

13. Remove the backing from the circle frame and stick the frame to the Lacé circle. Smooth it down with the folding tool.

14. Position the purple border near the left-hand edge of the raspberry card. Trim off the excess at top and bottom and stick the scraps to the backing for later. Repeat near the right-hand edge. Apply the pink strips in the same way, in the centre of the purple strips.

15. Dot high tack glue on the back of the Lacé circle, behind the rubber-stamped frame, using a scoring tool. Place it centrally on the card and stick it down.

16. Punch the corners of the raspberry and the dark purple card with a 3mm (1/8 in) single hole punch.

17. Place Peel-Off eyelets on the punched holes.

18. Punch out daisies from leftover rubber stamped paper. Place pink Peel-Off eyelet daisies in the centres. Peel off the backing and stick the daisies to the lady's hair.

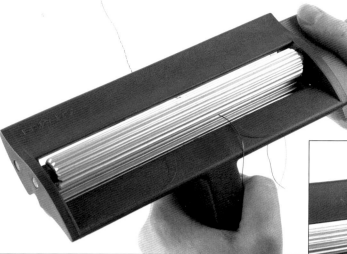

19. Stick 3D foam squares to the back of the lady. Peel off the backing and stick her down.

20. Cut 40cm (14in) of purple wire with wire cutters, and run it through a crimper with a metal cog – one with a plastic cog will be damaged by the wire.

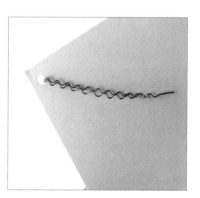

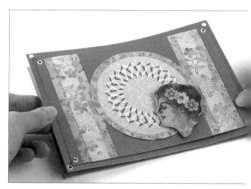

21. Bend the crimped wire 2.5cm (1in) down its length, fold it over and trim to create four hairpin shapes. Feed these through the eyelet holes to attach the raspberry card to the dark purple card.

22. Fold over the hairpin shapes to secure them at the back.

23. Place 3D foam squares on the back of the dark purple card, either side of each wire attachment and elsewhere, and mount this artwork on the light purple pearlescent card.

Opposite
The finished Old Shanghai card. Rubber stamping adds such a dramatic and personal flavour to your greetings cards. One stamp can be adapted to suit many themes simply by changing the ink colour. Hand colouring and stamping your background papers gives that ultimate individual touch. Here the sumptuous, oriental feel created by the printed vellum is complemented by floral stamping, and the lady adds the final air of decadence!

When you combine rubber stamps with Lacé, the possibilities are endless. From this whimsical butterfly card and gift tag, or the masculine paisley bookmark and card set, to the oriental-looking panel card and bookmark, each unique creation will stand out on the over-crowded mantelpiece.

Memory Lane Tag Book

I am an avid traveller, and photographs are my way of capturing special moments, crazy adventures and spectacular sites. They also allow me to take with me precious visual reminders of those I am parted from, however briefly.

This project is a mixture of basic book-making techniques, collage and creative machine stitching, allowing you to surround your photographs with delicate Lacé frames and preserve them in a beautiful tag book. I am sure that as you read this, a photograph has sprung to mind that deserves this special treatment. Go and dig it out and join me on a wonderful creative journey.

You will need

Lacé templates 33 and 12, knife and blades, score and fold tool, ruler and cutting mat

Low tack tape

Two aqua and two turquoise duo card tags, 203 x 64mm (8 x 2½in)

Two aqua and two turquoise duo card luggage labels, 82 x 38mm (3¼ x 1½in)

Scrap aqua and turquoise duo card

A4 lozenge printed vellum

Sewing machine

Paper scissors

18 gauge wire, wire cutters and round-nosed pliers

Plastic tube

Velvet ribbon in two shades

Double-sided tape

Circle and flower craft punches

Embroidery thread and heart-shaped button

3D foam squares

Landscape-shaped photograph

1. Place the lozenge-patterned vellum on the cutting mat, tape down template 33 and cut.

2. Fold back the cut shapes. Trim round the Lacé area leaving a 12mm (½in) border. Repeat to make a total of four vellum panels. Set aside.

36

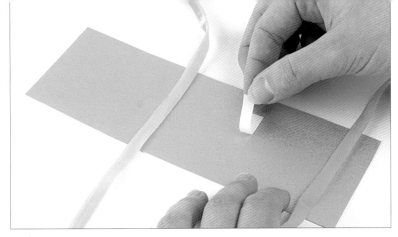

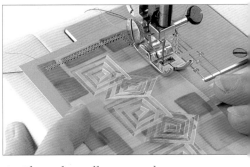

3. Cut two 61cm (24in) lengths of velvet ribbon in different shades. Stick a piece of double-sided tape on an aqua tag, 7.6cm (3in) from the top. Place a second piece 5cm (2in) lower down. Stick the ribbons on velvet-side down, 18cm (7in) from the end of each ribbon. Attach a turquoise tag further along the ribbon to the left, leaving a 1½cm (½in) gap between tags, and repeat with the other aqua and turquoise tags (see the diagram below).

4. Place the vellum panel centrally on a turquoise tag, over the ribbons, and stitch it in place using a sewing machine and turquoise thread. Repeat for the other three panels.

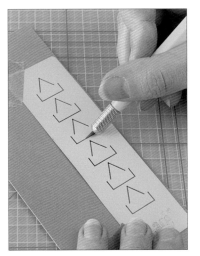

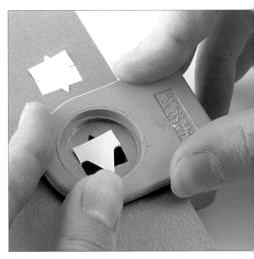

5. On a turquoise luggage label, make marks 38mm (1½in) down the length and use these as a guide to snip the corners, creating the distinctive label shape. Repeat on the other three luggage labels.

6. Place and secure the flip and fold bookmark template number 12 on scrap aqua card. Cut one shape, skip the next one and cut the third. Repeat on turquoise card.

7. Push the point down, flip it over and secure it. Place the circular craft punch around it upside down as shown, and punch to make a photo corner.

8. Make two photo corners in each colour and attach each one to a luggage label in the opposite colour.

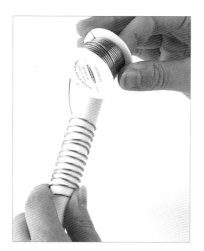

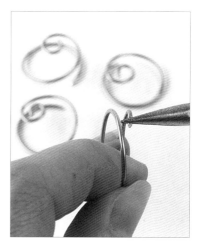

9. Take a length of 18 gauge turquoise wire, wrap it round an old plastic tube ten times and squeeze the wraps together to tighten the coil.

10. Snip off coils using wire cutters, to make jump rings.

11. Use round-nosed pliers to curl one end of each jump ring.

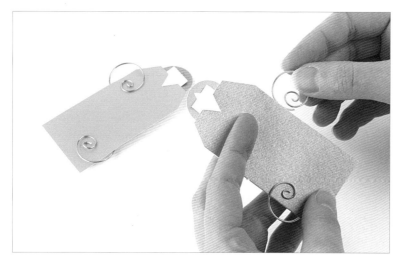

12. Clip the jump rings on to the luggage labels as shown.

13. Punch out a vellum daisy. Tear a bit of complementary coloured vellum and a bit of turquoise card, making sure you tear towards you.

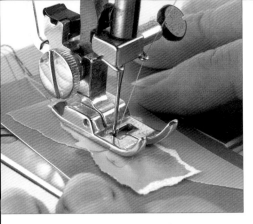

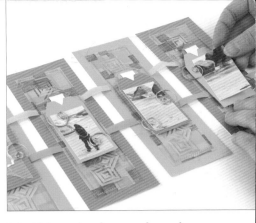

14. Layer these three items to create a collage and use a sewing machine and straight stitch to sew them to the front of a luggage label.

15. Use 3D foam squares to stick the luggage label to the tag on the far left. Tie a length of thread to a heart-shaped button and stick it to your collage with high tack glue.

16. Take a landscape-shaped photograph and cut it into strips 38mm x 63mm(1½in x 2½in). Place the strips of photograph behind the jump rings on your luggage labels.

What a wonderful way to capture a special moment or person. Folded, the tag book makes a personal keepsake. It can also be opened and framed to make a picture gift. When I look at this tag book, I can't help being taken back to the time and place where the photograph was taken, and I have used colours and embellishments to enhance these impressions. I can almost smell the sea, feel the sand underfoot and remember all the wishes I made on that magical beach in Western Australia years ago.

We all have photographs with stories to tell, stashed in shoe boxes or lost in albums. I invite you to take them out and draw inspiration from them. What colours, patterns and textures would bring them to life? Then I dare you to scour craft shops for appropriate papers, scrounge a sewing machine and spend time reliving those precious moments and framing them as they deserve.

Design your own template

The ultimate Lacé technique challenge is to create your own designs. All the existing templates have evolved from template 35, the dot pattern template shown on the facing page.

Your challenge is to take template 35 and follow the steps to create Lacé designs of your own. You can be as creative or innovative as you like.

I recommend setting aside some time to play with this template: start by perforating the holes on to white card blanks. Take a pencil and experiment with matching up the dots. When you have developed a design that appeals to you, you are ready to create your own template. Good luck!

You will need

Lacé templates 14 and 35, knife and spare blades, score and fold tool, ruler and cutting mat

Low tack tape

Lacé paper pricking tool

Paper pricking mat

Pencil

Scrap card

A4 white pearlescent card

Square white pearlescent card blank, 12 x 12cm (4¾ x 4¾in)

Mulberry glitter duo card

Large and small heart craft punches

3D foam squares

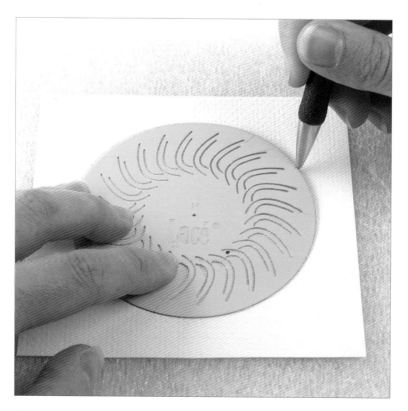

1. Position template 14 on scrap card over the paper pricking mat. Make a pencil mark through the centre hole. Then trace around the template with a pencil.

  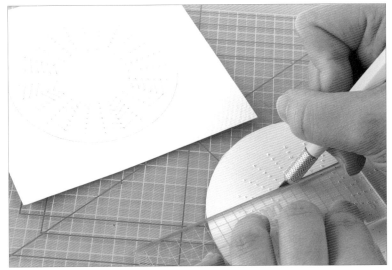

2. Use the centre mark to position template 35 over the pencil circle and secure it with low tack tape. Prick through it with the paper pricking tool, starting at twelve o'clock.

3. Use a pencil to draw your own design for a template, using the holes as a guide.

4. You now have a template design, but you cannot cut and use this as a template because pencil marks will come through it. Keep it as a reference to help you prick and cut your Lacé artwork.

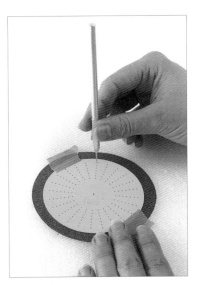 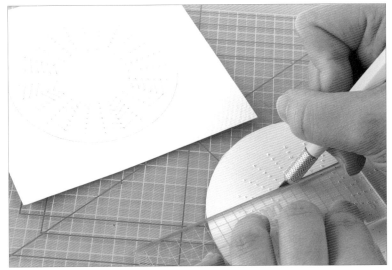

5. Take the mulberry piece of duo card and cut round the larger template to make a circle. Position the smaller template and prick the holes as you did before.

6. Take off the Lacé template, turn over to the white side of the card and using your design as a guide, use the Lacé ruler, which has a metal edge, and the Lacé knife to cut the lines.

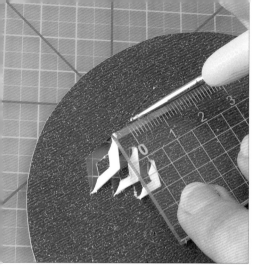

7. Score lines from dot to dot and flip up the V-shapes.

8. Fold back the V-shapes with the other end of the score and fold tool, and set the Lacé circle aside.

9. Punch out nine large hearts from white pearlescent card and nine small hearts from mulberry card, and stick the small hearts to the large hearts using a dot of high tack glue on each.

10. Stick 3D foam squares to the back of the large hearts and place them on the Lacé circle as shown.

11. Use 3D foam squares to attach the Lacé artwork to your pearlescent white card blank.

The finished card. Keeping your colour palette restricted to two colours creates a sophisticated feel to this gorgeous card. The addition of my favourite punched shapes in matching tones frames the card to perfection.

Designing your own templates takes a little extra time but gives a great sense of achievement. With these cards, most of the effect is achieved by the design of the templates – the colour schemes are simple and a mere sprinkling of embellishments is enough to complete the look.

Index